The authors, artist, and publisher wish to thank the following for their invaluable advice and instruction for this book:

Jane Hyman, B.S., M. Ed. (Reading), M. Ed. (Special Needs), Ed. D. (candidate)

Rose Feinberg, B.S., M. Ed. (Elementary Education), Ed. D. (Reading and Language Arts)

R.L. 1.8 Spache

Published by Ideals Publishing Corporation
Nashville, Tennessee 37214

Printed and bound in the United States of America.

Library of Congress Cataloging-in-Publication Data

Berger, Melvin.
    The whole world in your hands: looking at maps/by Melvin and Gilda Berger; illustrated by Robert Quackenbush.
        p.   cm. — (Discovery readers)
    Summary: Explains what maps are and how to use them, discusses map symbols and their meanings, and includes maps of a house, community, city, state, country, and the world.
    ISBN 0-8249-8646-6 (lib. bdg.)—ISBN 0-8249-8609-1 (pbk.)
    1. Maps—Juvenile literature. [1. Maps.] I. Berger, Gilda.
II. Quackenbush, Robert M., ill. III. Title. IV. Series.
GA105.6.B47   1993
912—dc20   92-18199
                                                                        CIP
                                                                         AC

Discovery Readers is a registered trademark of Ideals Publishing Corporation.

Produced by Barish International, New York.

Here's a map.
It's a map of the world.
The world is thousands of miles
across.
Yet it fits on this map.

Pick up the map.
Now you've the whole world in
your hands!

A map is a picture.
It shows a place as it looks from
up high.
A map makes big distances look
small.

Maps may show the whole world.
Or they may show
    —one country
    —one state
    —one city
    —one community
    —even one house!

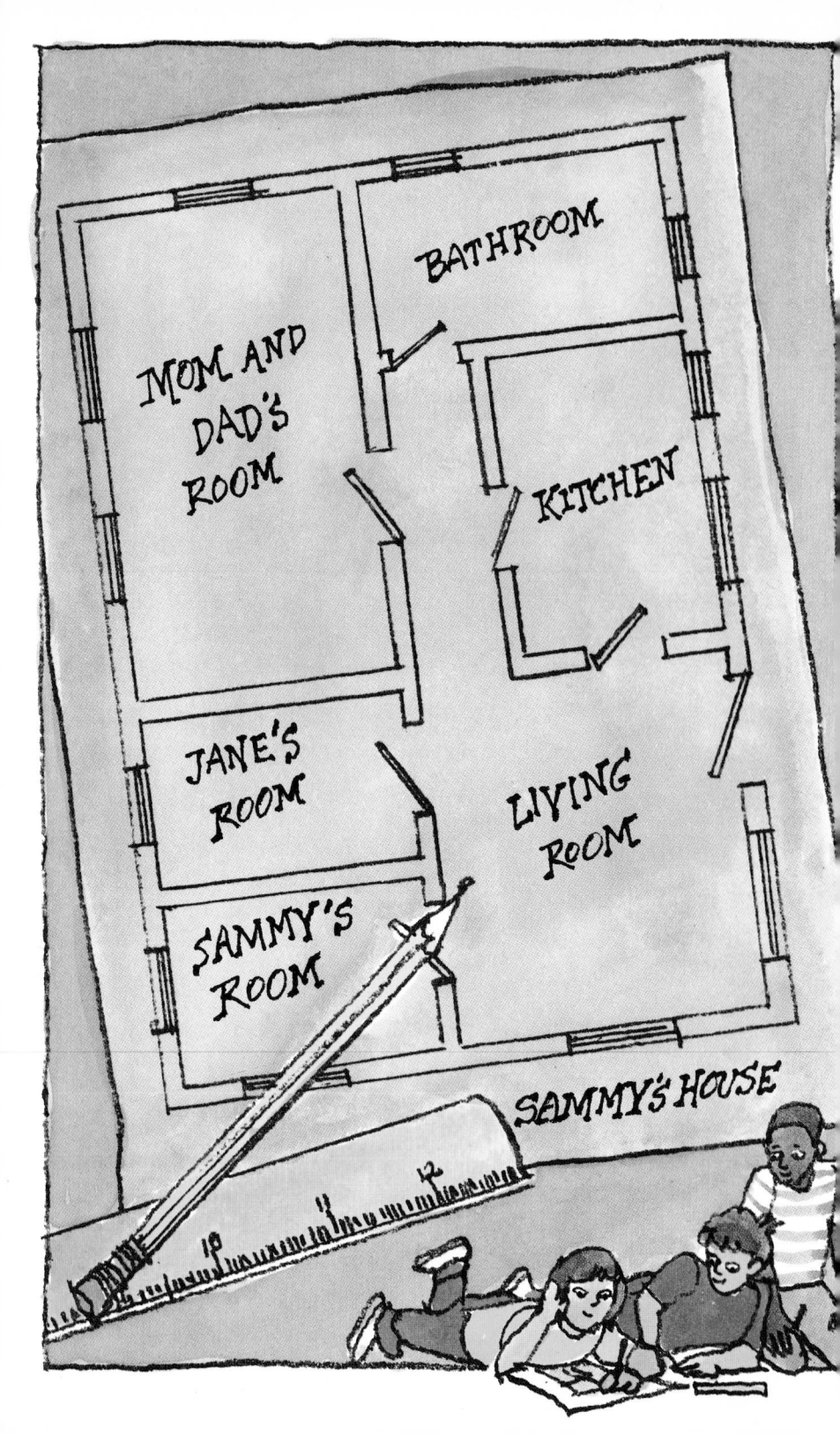

Here's a map of Sammy's house.
It shows Sammy's room.
His sister Jane's room.
Mom and Dad's room.

Whose room is near Sammy's room?
Whose room is far from Sammy's
    room?

Sammy's house has other rooms
    —a living room
    —a kitchen
    —a bathroom.

Can you find each room?

Sammy and Jane have alarm clocks.
Their alarms ring at 7:30 every
school day.
The brother and sister race to the
bathroom.
Each wants to be first.
Jane usually wins.
Can you see why?

Sammy's house is in a community
called Twin Oaks.
This is a map of his community.
Sammy's house is on Second Street.
Do you see it?

All the streets in Twin Oaks run up
and down.
Up and down on a map means
north and south.

Move up on a map and you go
north.
Move down on a map and you go
south.

All the avenues run from side to
side.
Side to side on a map means east
and west.

Move right on a map and you go
east.
Move left on a map and you go
west.

Most maps have four arrows off to
the side.
The arrows show the four directions—

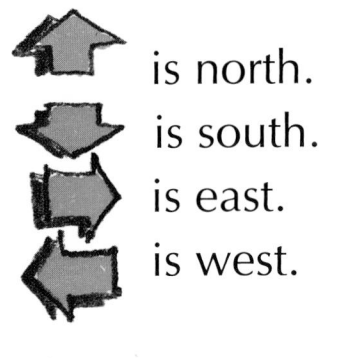 is north.
is south.
is east.
is west.

Sammy's best friend also lives on
Second Street.
His name is Jimmy.
Jimmy lives between Pine Avenue
and Oak Avenue.

Sammy often plays at Jimmy's
house.
Jimmy lives south of Sammy.
To get to Jimmy's house, Sammy
walks south on Second Street.

Sammy and Jimmy walk to school
together.
Jimmy walks north on Second Street
to Sammy's house.

Together they go east on Elm
   Avenue.
Then they turn north on Fourth
   Street.
The school is right there.
Can you trace their way with your
   finger?

Every Saturday Sammy goes to the library.

He walks south on Second Street to Pine Avenue.

He turns east and walks to Fourth Street.

At Fourth Street, he turns south.

Trace Sammy's path with your finger.

Can you figure out how Sammy
  walks
  —to the post office
  —to the railroad station
  —to the supermarket?

Twin Oaks is in a small city called Westover.

This map shows the town's main roads.

North Highway is north of the town. South Highway is south. West Highway is on the west side. East Highway is to the east.

The map also shows some important places in Westover
—the airport
—the fairgrounds
—the zoo
—the ballpark
—the movie theater
—two shopping malls.

One day Sammy's family went to the
    fairgrounds.
Sammy's mother drove.

First she went east on Elm Avenue.
Then she turned south on East
    Highway.
Finally she parked at the fairgrounds.
Sammy and Jane tried all the rides.

FAIRGROUNDS

TICKETS

Each summer Grandma comes to
  visit.
Sammy's dad goes to meet her.
He drives to the airport.

First Dad heads north on Second
  Street.
Next he turns east on North
  Highway.
When he gets to East Highway, he
  turns north.
He follows that road to the airport.

Sammy's town could be anywhere.
Let's pretend it's in the state of
    Kansas.
Kansas is right in the middle of the
    United States.

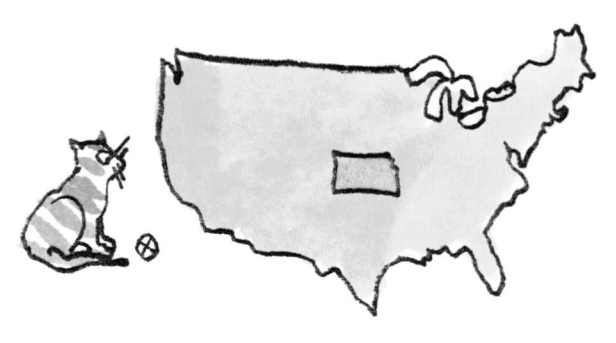

Here is a map of Kansas.
The dots show the cities.
The bigger the dot, the bigger the
    city.
Can you find three big cities in
    Kansas?
Wichita is the biggest city in Kansas.
Nearly half a million people live in
    Wichita.

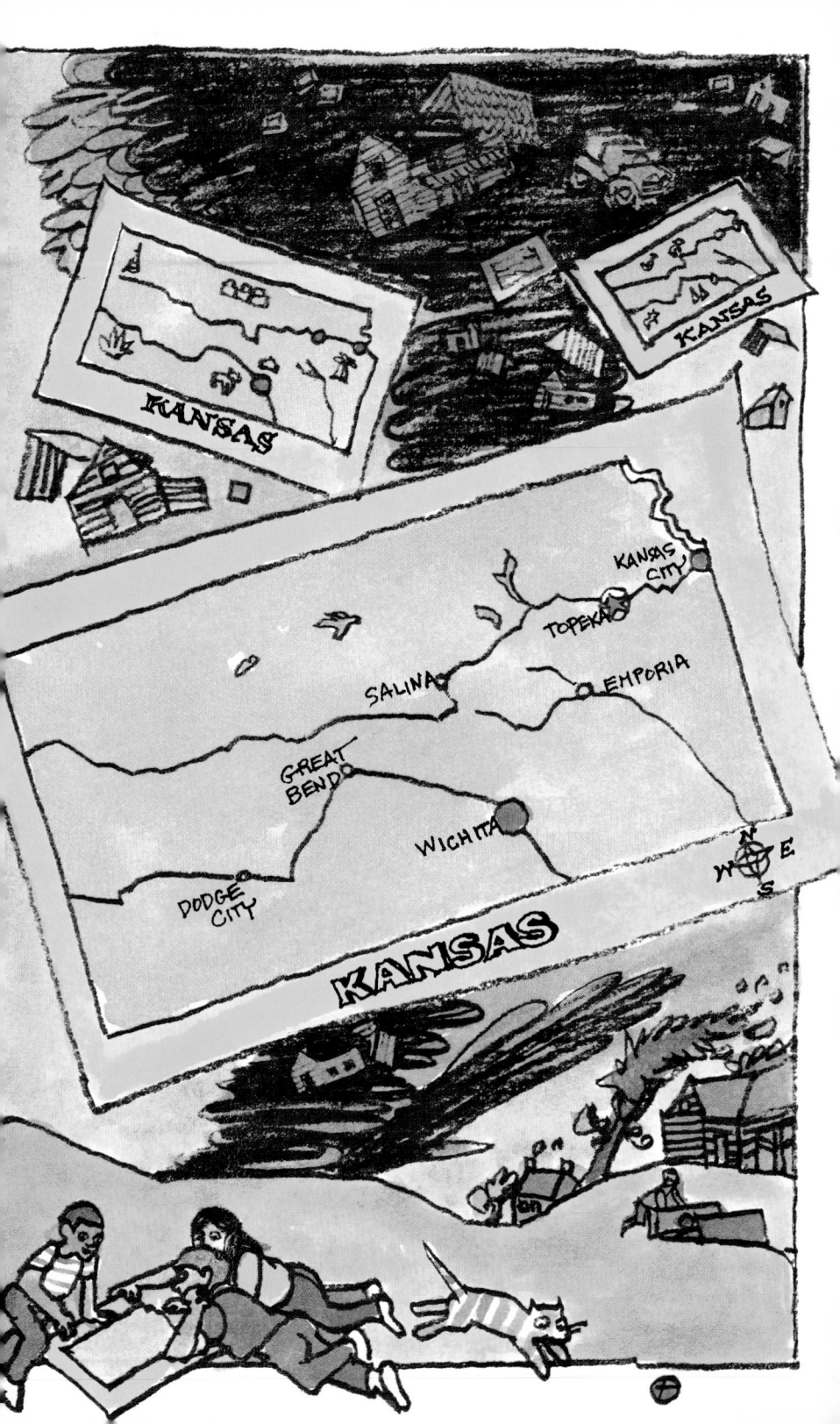

KANSAS

KANSAS

KANAS
CITY

TOPEKA

EMPORIA

SALINA

GREAT
BEND

WICHITA

DODGE
CITY

N
W E
S

KANSAS

Next to the Wichita dot is a drawing
of small airplanes in a factory.
The drawing is a symbol.
It tells you that people in Wichita
build small airplanes.
Many people in this city work in
airplane factories.
Others do different kinds of work.

26

Kansas City is in the northeast
corner of Kansas.

The city is only about half as big as
Wichita.

So Kansas City has a smaller dot on
the map.

Topeka is just west of Kansas City.
It is the smallest of the big cities in
Kansas.

Topeka has a star inside a dot.
A star is the symbol of a capital city.
Topeka is the capital of Kansas.

The governor of Kansas lives and
    works in Topeka.
Many others who live in Topeka also
    work for the state.

There's much more to Kansas than
    its cities.
A lot goes on in the rest of the state.

Do you see the sheaves of wheat in
the west part of Kansas?
This symbol shows that farmers
grow wheat all around here.
Kansas farmers grow more wheat
than farmers in any other state.

Kansas farmers also raise chickens,
sheep, and cattle.
Look for tiny symbols of these
animals on the map.
These symbols show where you can
find most of the animal farms.

The northwest part of the map
　　shows oil well symbols.
Lots of oil lies under the ground
　　here.

Move south on the map.
Go to the southwest corner of
　　Kansas.
Here you see pictures of flames.
Workers pump natural gas from this
　　area.

Head east across the map.
Do you see little cars loaded with
   coal?
It's easy to guess what happens here.
Coal miners dig for coal in deep
   tunnels.

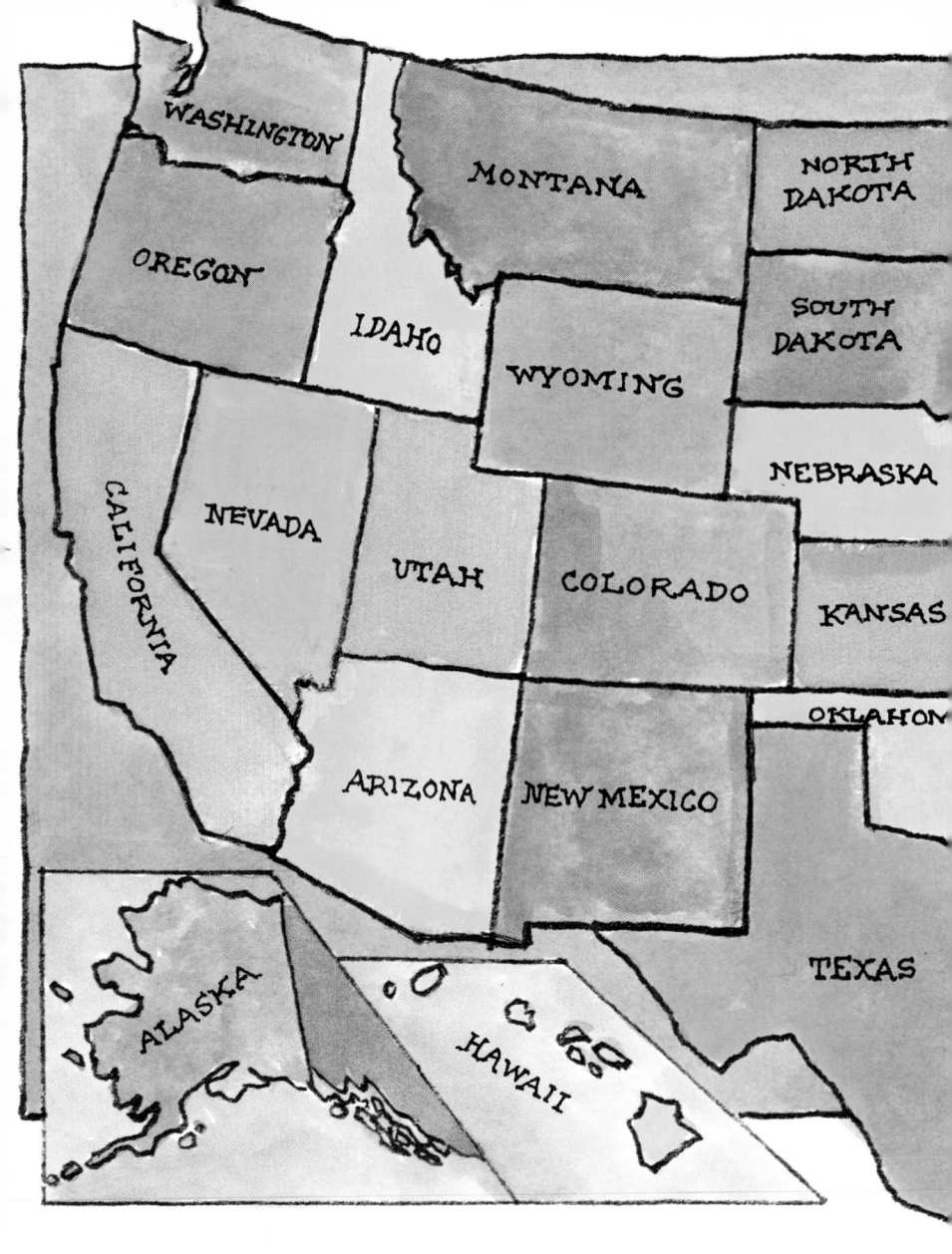

Kansas is one state in the United
    States.
The United States has fifty states.

Here is a map of our whole country.
Can you find Kansas?
Can you find your state?

33

There are about 150 countries in the whole world.

The countries are spread out over seven continents—Asia, Africa, North America, South America, Antarctica, Australia, and Europe.

Between the continents are four main oceans—Atlantic, Pacific, Indian, and Arctic.

This map shows the continents and oceans of the world.

This map is like the first map in the book.
They are both maps of the world.
Yet there is one big difference.

The map in the front makes the world look flat.
This map shows that the world is round.
The world is really as round as a globe.

An orange is also as round as a
    globe.
Imagine a map of the world on the
    orange skin.

Peel off the orange skin in one big
    piece.

Push the skin flat on a table.

The orange-skin map would look
    like this map.

Take a close look at the map.
Can you find South America?

Find the line marked equator. It is like a belt around the middle of the world.

North of the equator is the northern half of the world.

South of the equator is the southern half of the world.

Near the equator:
　　Every day is like a summer day.
　　People wear light clothes to keep
　　　　cool.
　　Trees and grass and flowers grow
　　　　all year long.
　　Plants grow quickly.
　　Sweet potatoes, peanuts, and
　　　　corn grow well.

Now find the North Pole on the
map.
It is far up in the north.

Find the South Pole.
It is far down in the south.
Did you know that the poles are the
coldest places in the world?

Near the poles:
    Every day is cold.
    There's lots of snow and ice.
    People wear heavy clothes to
        keep warm.
    Few animals or plants live or
        grow on the land.

Here almost all living things are
    found in the seas.

Not many people live near the
  poles.
And few live near the equator.

Most people live in places in
  between.

In those places, the weather is
  mild.
Usually it is not very hot or very
  cold.
Some people live where the soil is
  rich.
These places are good for farming.

Some people live near big forests.
Many cut trees for lumber.

Some people live near oceans or
　　rivers.
Many catch and eat lots of seafood.

Some people live where there is oil
　　under the ground.
Many drill for oil and ship it out.

Some people live in big cities.
Many work in factories and offices.

A map can tell many things
    —the work people do
    —the foods they eat
    —the clothes they wear
    —the kinds of houses they live in.

Maps are wonderful tools.
They help bring us all closer
    together.

Index